God is Pro-Choice

GOD

IS

PRO-CHOICE

This book is dedicated

to all of God's lost lambs.

Don't worry, he will find us all.

I would like to thank Clipart.com and other royalty-free providers of photos and clipart. None of the art used in this book has been changed substantially from the original. I did reduce color items to black and white to contain printing costs, and I have combined some items.

Title: God is Pro-Choice

Author: William Taylor

Cover Design: Eastland Enterprises, Inc.

ISBN: 978-0-615-35703-4

First Edition, December 2009

GOD IS PRO CHOICE

Sometimes there are no good choices, but we still must choose.

William Taylor

www.thelonelyliberal.com

Eastland Enterprises

Preface

Please be aware that this is not a story with plots and twists and turns. It is a compilation of 19 short essays. You will find some characters and some conflicts about real people and real circumstances. Each section is short so as not to bore you too much. If one section does not agree with you just skip to the next section. Each section has its own distinct story. This book is a quick read. I could have made it longer but I don't like to stretch things out.

I would like to take one moment to communicate for whom I am writing this book. One of the reasons I wrote this book was for the many people who want to understand why there is a Pro-choice movement. Although I feel that abortion should be kept safe and legal, we must all recognize that it is not a desirable situation to be in. It is not true that the pro-life people are the only ones who feel negatively about abortion. Everyone feels badly about abortion. This book is an effort, on my part, to introduce readers to other perspectives and considerations related to this issue. If we can come to a more complete understanding of what might be involved in the lives of those who go through this experience, maybe we can more understand why this is not a simple (right or wrong) issue and there are no easy answers to this problem. Whether abortion is kept legal or made illegal, there is more to this topic than meets the eye. There is a second reason I wrote this book. I wrote it for myself. This is a subject that I have had some limited experience with. It is my hope that I can make a contribution by sharing my limited but honest insight on this very misunderstood topic.

Table of Contents

Introduction

A storm is brewing in our courts as the twenty-first century gets underway. If one or two more conservative Justices are appointed to the Supreme Court, the legal status of women will likely change. Women should know that their freedom may be at risk. They may be legally forced to bear a child, even when that child is conceived as a result of rape.

We need to swing left, or progressive (liberal and/or Democrat), and stay progressive until our future presidents have appointed more liberal judges to what is quickly becoming the Supreme (Kangaroo) Court, a court that rubber-stamps the agenda of American conservatives. I'm not trying to be an alarmist, but I'm sure that God doesn't consider all extinguishing of life unnecessary, and that he certainly does consider the birth of some children wrong. The decision whether to abort a pregnancy should remain between the woman and God. Women concerned with preserving the rights and independence of women should put on their liberal hat as they go into the voting booth, until women are again safe from the new, twisted justice being shaped by the US Supreme Court. Only by voting for more liberal Senators, who will act to confirm more liberal Justices, can women fight the conservative trend of the recent Court. Only this way can they be sure that their bodies, and the right to decide what they do with them, remain between them and God.

The issue of abortion has touched my life in a way that changed me forever. This may sound strange coming from a man, but the experience of being linked to just one abortion taught me more than I ever wanted to learn about the subject. I now understand my experience to be a "life lesson," a cruel, humbling lesson. I had until then taken life as a joke, and now it's my life that has become the joke. I'm not going to explain that last statement --- I'm sure some of you already understand. For anyone who doesn't, I only hope, for your sake, that you never will.

This book has 19 sections; each presents a reason why abortion should be kept safe and legal. You may be wondering how there could be so many reasons abortions are performed. Well, there are probably even more, but these reasons are drawn from my (limited) experience with such matters. The crux of the issue is judgment. Those who would push to make abortions illegal have a flaw in their reasoning. They're wearing blinders, and it often seems that all they can do is dogmatically repeat their mantras: "Life is precious." "It's murder." "The fetus is a life." "It's an innocent child."

The list of such platitudes goes on and on. Of course, if it really were as simple as that, we would all be in agreement, and there would be no debate about abortion. I don't doubt that most pro-lifers are well meaning people, but I believe that their goals are wrong. If the issue were that simple, that black and white, there would never have been a *Roe v. Wade* ruling, a ruling that even today continues to generate intense feelings, controversy, and drama, in America and all over the world. Pro-lifers' principles and platitudes are malicious and hurtful, aimed even at victims of rape and sexual extortion; these tenets are meaningless to any young girl who has been a victim of incestuous molestation. It's not reasonable to expect such women to want these children, or to willingly live in the same world with them. As I will demonstrate later, God himself killed an innocent newborn child because it was the result of crime and sin.

The so-called "right-to-lifers" believe that many women are promiscuous bed-hoppers, involved in a hedonistic love fest, too busy having sex to take birth control pills. They have lumped all women seeking abortions in that category. But no one can discern others' lives and situations with enough accuracy to make such sweeping judgments; "right-to-lifers" are no more capable than anyone else of judging whether a woman is virtuous, or promiscuous, or mentally ill.

Many self-identified Christians cannot even discern whether their own ministers are gay, *e.g.,* Ted Haggard (allegedly), once the leader of the thirty-million-strong National Association of Evangelicals. I have no problem with homosexuals, but it seems rather hypocritical for an allegedly gay man to preach an anti-gay, "family values" message. Many so-called conservative Christians cannot discern when their ministers are (apparently) lechers, such as Jimmy Swaggart, or thieves, such as Jim Bakker. They can't discern whether the people they vote for are gay --- *e.g.,* Senator Larry Craig (apparently caught trying to "hook up" in an airport restroom) or even a borderline pedophile --- *e.g.,* Congressman Mark Foley (accused of sending explicit sexual messages to minors). And while we're at it, let's not forget Congressman Randy "Duke" Cunningham, who (it seems) admitted influence-peddling to the tune of $2.4 million, and at least four Republican legislators who became targets of Justice Department inquiries in the wake of the Jack Abramoff scandal.

What I really want to say to such right-to-life conservative Christians is this: please set your own house in order first, before you judge others. You have followed the lecherous and the gay, and still called yourself righteous. You have voted for one corrupt Congressman after another. Your judgment cannot be as good as you seem to think it is! When women are forced to consider the horrible decision of abortion, they need your prayers, not your condescending attitude (may God please be with us all).

Let's go over what you should expect from this book. On occasion, you may get a feeling of déjà vu as you read. This is because the same ideas are repeated, in the beginning, to reinforce a position. Try not to balk at the words "abortion," "right-to-life," "pro-choice," and so forth. It's necessary to use these words frequently; this is a narrow subject and there isn't a broad range of vocabulary on this issue. I could have cited more research and material from other people's books and ideas, going on for another hundred pages, but I hope to make this a quick read. The images are included to enhance the text for more visually oriented people, and to reinforce the textual points.

So much for the literary "housekeeping" involved with this book. Back to the subject at hand.

Some who call themselves Christians seem hell-bent on making abortion illegal. They know the Republican Party needs them for its very survival; although some more moderate, mainstream Republicans view many right-to-lifers as crackpots, the fact remains that the GOP cannot survive without their votes. The problem the conservatives have is that America, as a whole, is pro-choice. To get around this problem, it often seems that the Republicans promise right-to-lifers appointments of Supreme Court Justices in exchange for the right-to-lifers' votes. To hell with what America wants, they seem to say. They intend to "back door" their laws into our lives, relying on the power of the bench to remedy what Congress has been unable to outlaw via legislation.

I was compelled to write this book because I see the high frequency of abortion as a symptom of a greater evil --- that we, as a nation, may become hell-bound, and not just some of our citizens. I believe the prevalence of abortion is telling us that something is very wrong with the fabric of our society, not just some members of it.

It often seems that Americans have short memories. It wasn't so long ago that abortion was illegal. We seem to have forgotten that we've already tried making abortion illegal, and it didn't work very well at the time. What makes people think it will work now? There may, in fact, be a way to rid the world of abortion, but there are some facts we must come to grips with first.

The first fact is that we must begin to attack the true problem. We have become accustomed to attacking symptoms rather than problems: when we have a headache, we take aspirin, and the headache goes away. However, we rarely attempt to deal with stress, which might be the real problem behind the symptom. The same is true of abortion. We know that far too many abortions are carried out today, so we pass laws to stop or reduce the number of abortions. But the real problems --- unwanted pregnancies, lack of parental planning --- are not addressed. We need to look at the real problems, and until we do, the symptom --- abortion --- will never go away. The entire pro-life movement is aiming at the wrong target. They should be addressing our inability to plan a family properly, and the trend toward promiscuity in the current generation.

Attacking abortion by addressing only the symptoms is like trying to kill a tree by plucking off its leaves. Perhaps it's time we try to uproot this tree --- abortion --- instead. To say only that abortion is wrong (or right) is simple-minded at best. It's quite possible that sometimes it is neither right nor wrong. This simple-minded approach, exhibited by many right-to-lifers, completely ignores the fact that **no one** enjoys having an abortion.

It also ignores the fact that we live in a mismanaged society. Our promiscuous, immoral culture must someday face the real problem: until we begin to teach sexual responsibility classes, along with sexual education classes, abortions will not stop. Until our television, radio, and print media stop flooding our children's minds with sexual material, abortions will not stop. Laws against drug abuse don't stop drug abuse; laws against drunk driving, murder, gang violence, and all other destructive behavior that people engage in don't stop such behavior. They just ensure that such laws will be broken by those who don't mind breaking the law. The law can't fix everything for us; first, we must fix ourselves, and then we will not need such laws.

Pro-life people can be righteous enough, what they stand for is a good cause. But sometimes it's not what we do see, but what we don't see. In this section, I'll go into what we often don't see, and then we can ask ourselves my question --- "Where's the beef?"

Where's the Beef

I feel that this first section, even more than later chapters of this book, is the strongest argument against pro-lifers. After this, a cooler, more restrained approach will be taken.

The road to hell, it is said, is paved with good intentions. This is a good way to state my opinion of the so-called "pro-life" movement. I'm sure they believe in their cause, just as I'm sure they believe in their righteousness. But they ignore too many facts surrounding this issue to be, finally, anything more than intolerant, delusional fascists. I see them on the news from time to time, carrying picket signs as they protest outside what they call abortion clinics. These signs often display pictures of the mutilated bodies of fetuses, and sport mottoes like "Abortion is murder," "Life is precious," and "Reverse *Roe v. Wade*." They assume, and then try to project, an image of righteousness. They obviously believe they're doing God's work. For a time, I was conflicted by their seemingly righteous cause, but something seemed amiss. I couldn't put my finger on it at first. Then one day I heard the question that summed up my feelings about the so-called "pro-lifers." The question was "Where's the beef?"

They organized themselves as a single entity, for one cause, protesting abortion. But we are surrounded by death, in every imaginable form --- our population is, in fact, a victim of systematic and institutionalized death (which I'll discuss in a moment). Yet these issues are not addressed by the "pro-lifers" in the same manner; indeed, they seem to ignore them altogether.
What do I mean by "systematic and institutionalized death"? Before I answer that, let me make just one point. The so called "pro-life" people have some strange political bedfellows. As you probably know, they are predominantly conservative Republicans. Why does this matter? For many years, most corporate political campaign contributions went to the Republican Party. These death merchants --- military-industrial corporations, big tobacco companies, and the National Rifle Association (NRA), among others --- helped keep Republicans in power. Working along with them were the pro-lifers and the self-styled Moral Majority.

My first point about the pro-lifers is this: the Bible says to avoid even the appearance of anything that might seem evil. Yet the Republican Party, the military-industrial complex, the NRA, the tobacco companies (who have alone arguably killed more people than Hitler), and the pro-lifers can all be found in the same political bed. So I ask: how can anyone side with death merchants, warmongers, and dispensers of cancer, and call oneself "pro-life"? Such people are not pro-life --- they are in fact **anti-choice**. These political bedfellows, including the military-industrial complex, may ultimately be responsible for the deaths of millions of people.

Jesus would not be their political partner. Jesus went into the temple and overturned the moneylenders' tables for doing business in the house of the Lord. How can people vote with the vendors of the instruments of death, yet believe themselves to be righteous?

Where's the beef? Some pro-lifers take the cheap and easy way out --- they call poor women, disillusioned women, raped and abused women, murderers. They fight against God's lost lambs. As a group, they offer the victims no useful help. They don't want to pay taxes for needed orphanages. They don't pool their money and buy shelters for these girls, who often have nowhere else to go when their parents discover their condition and throw them out of the house. They're mostly about lip service, self-righteously preaching "tough love." But where's the beef? The cruelest part of the right-to-life movement is their marching in front of clinics, further traumatizing women who may have been raped or molested. If that's the best they can do, if that's all they can offer, they should just stay home.

When the right-to-lifers had a chance to prove they were really pro-life, they came up empty. Recently, roughly 40 million Americans were without health insurance, and nearly 45,000 people died annually because they lacked any form of health insurance. The "right-to-lifers" didn't care. They whined about their taxes going up, even though raising taxes can help reduce the national deficit. Even today, they piss and moan that the government might get too big, as an excuse for remaining selfish, while their Christian brothers and sisters die of simple neglect in the so-called greatest country on earth. As long as they can march in front of clinics and degrade others as sluts and murderers, they're happy with themselves. But when it comes time to put up real money, they do nothing. If I, with a broken-down jalopy in my garage and a home badly in need of repair, am willing to pay more taxes to save some lives --- and I am pro-choice --- what is their problem? They are not pro-life. If they are, let them prove it. Because it looks as though they're only pro-life as long as it's free, or cheap, to be pro-life. If they were really pro-life, they would show the world by getting off their fat wallets and purses and proving it.

I'm not much of a Bible-thumper, but before we go any further, let me quote Jesus just once. If it's OK to pray before a football game, I think now might also be an appropriate time. So let me just say this:

Our Father in heaven,

hallowed be Your name.

Your kingdom come.

Your will be done on earth, as it is in heaven.

Give us this day our daily bread.

And forgive us our debts,

as we forgive our debtors.

And do not lead us into temptation,

but deliver us from the evil one.

For Yours is the kingdom

and the power

and the glory

forever.

Amen.

A picture is worth a thousand words. If Jesus could forgive those who hung him on the cross, why can't some people forgive those who have unfortunately found themselves feeling they should seek abortions? Let's not forget that God will have the last word. So instead of persecuting these people for their sins, let us pray for their souls.

Section

1

I have a question for those who call themselves "pro-life," who believe we should pass laws making abortion illegal. Who died and made you God? First, if you're a man, you don't have much to say on this issue --- it is the woman's life that will be affected, much more than yours. She's the one who will have to bear and raise the child, or have to live with the consequences of aborting the child. It is her body that will be used or misused. It is her life that will be most changed. Many men nevertheless believe they should be able to decide for women whether it should be legal or illegal for them to have abortions. But if the shoe were on the other foot, how would men react? Imagine that the women of America banded together and voted to prevent unwanted pregnancies by passing a law requiring all men to get temporary vasectomies until they're financially ready to care for their children. The male population of America would be outraged. It's all too easy for men to pass laws that only women can be guilty of breaking. Making abortion illegal does not present any danger to men, but women who feel compelled to have an abortion anyway, and women who are pressured by men to have abortions, are at much greater risk if abortion is outlawed.

One of the many Christian programs on television showed a group of people who risked arrest to prevent fetuses from being aborted. These "rescue teams" had been trained to infiltrate security / police cordons, and try to talk mothers-to-be out of having abortions. It was good to see that so many people cared enough to try to make a difference, but I have a reservation about such efforts. These people, in pursuing this tactic, show up only for a brief moment in these women's lives, and try to help them make decisions that will affect the rest of their lives. In some cases, these "rescuers" might in fact help some women to make good decisions. But just as surely, they may be enabling bad decisions.

These "rescuers" may think they're helping women when they talk them out of having abortions. But when the "rescuers" go back home, and pat themselves on the back for a job well done, the mother-to-be is alone once more. She still has her original problem; she will soon be having her baby. When her pregnancy becomes obvious to others, when her parents realize she's pregnant, where will the "rescuers" be when she's kicked out of the only home she's ever known, and is forced to resort to welfare? Where will the "rescuers" be when an irate parent finds out his daughter has been sexually active, and beats the girl half to death? Where will the "rescuers" be when they've made some woman feel so guilty about contemplating abortion that she commits suicide, and two lives are lost instead of one? It's easy to "rescue" for a minute, or for a day. But maybe we shouldn't interfere in these women's business if we're not going to be around to pick up the pieces afterward. Good intentions can be of great value, but this may not be enough --- good intentions can sometimes do more harm than good.

If everyone agreed not to have abortions, and all the unwanted children were put up for adoption, what would we do when the orphanages were filled to overflowing? What would we do when there weren't enough foster parents to go around? We'll have a "stockpile" of unwanted children on our hands, and these children will likely be cooped up in large buildings, virtual warehouses, where they'll have the quality of life of caged animals. Such institutions will also breed tomorrow's criminals. Where will the "rescuers" be then? They may be the very ones who don't want such institutions in their neighborhoods.

Some of these children, the lucky ones, will find parents who will love them and raise them to be good Christians. For the rest, life will be much like reform school. The state and federal governments will have to raise taxes to build these institutions, and (as with all government projects) far more money will go into the bureaucracy of paper-pushers running the program than will go to benefit the children.

I wonder what's wrong with this world. Many of these very same Christians, who would outlaw abortion in the name of God, contribute to the destruction of breathing, walking, talking human beings. Our taxes are used to build bombs and support wars that have killed human beings on a wholesale basis. I don't see the same concern for these victims of overt warfare that they claim to have for the unborn. People starve in the streets of America, and again the right-to-lifers lack concern for these unfortunates. I cannot believe in the professed concern of the so-called "pro-lifers," not until I see them show the same concern for those already born.

I know what some readers may be thinking --- even if these children are warehoused, they will at least be alive. This is right, up to a point. But consider that life, true life, is more than just breathing and eating.

Time is running out for us all, and surely we all want to see at least some of today's problems resolved before our days are done. The time will come when we must take a long, honest look at the problems we face today. Abortion is temporary, but if we make it illegal, that long, honest look required to resolve the issue won't happen now, but later, sometime in the future. Let's leave the law as it is, and give ourselves time to resolve the problem. Let's declare war on the things that contribute to unwanted pregnancies, and rid ourselves of these things.

Section 2: Temporary Condition

By now I'm sure you've realized that I'm very much in favor of keeping abortion safe and legal. But I don't feel that this should be a permanent solution. In my opinion, we should keep it safe and legal until we find a way to train ourselves and our children to effectively prevent unwanted pregnancies and all their causes. We know that the main cause of unwanted pregnancies is ignorance, and the problem is only compounded by such reprehensible behaviors as rape, incest, child molestation and abuse, peer pressure, and sexual harassment, to name a few. The point is that it's better to keep abortion legal, until we can find some answers to these problems, than to make it illegal and never deal with the root causes because we fail to come to terms with the problems openly and honestly.

We must, however, emphasize the word "temporary," to convey the urgency of finding a solution to this problem. An analogy that may prove useful here has to do with a method I know for discouraging children from lying. Just as with abortion, we're confronted with an unwanted behavior, lying. We have two choices --- we can either outlaw lying or we can deal with it more openly. If we make lying illegal, then obviously no one will admit to lying; it will remain a hidden problem, difficult to address. On the other hand, let's imagine that one parent does **not** forbid lying, having an effective plan for correcting the child who shows such behavior. This is how the plan works: when the child lies, the parent promises the child something the child has wanted for a long time, and promises to give the item on a specific date (one the parent knows the child will remember). When the time comes, the parent conveniently "forgets" about it. It's important to make sure the child is old enough to remember the original lie, the transgression that incurs this treatment. When the child confronts the parent with the parent's broken promise (apparently a lie), the parent reminds the child of the original lie, and points out that if the child can lie, then it should be OK for the parent to lie also. This may have to be done more than once, but after a time, the child begins to realize that it's painful to be lied to, and that it must therefore be wrong to lie. If the parent had told the child that lying would be punished, the child would be much more careful to hide any future lies. And perhaps the child would grow significantly older before the parent could finally show the child how wrong it is to lie.

The moral of the story is this: if an unwanted behavior is simply "illegal," the parent may not catch such behavior as soon, or may not be able to impart the lesson as early, if in fact it's not too late altogether. Now which do you believe is the better way to deal with unwanted behavior? Is it better to make threats of punishment, or try to deal with the problem openly --- trying to make the source of the problem go away, or just the unwanted behavior (the symptom)?

Let's look at another unwanted behavior. Say that drinking alcoholic beverages is illegal. We know alcohol is dangerous, and under certain circumstances even deadly. Let's also say we find it difficult to control the use of alcohol, and let's look at both the illegal and the legal methods of dealing with the problem. When the consumption of alcohol was illegal, during Prohibition, people like Al Capone and his hit man, Frank Nitti, ruled a vast empire illegally trafficking in alcohol. Hundreds of millions of dollars were put into the hands of a man who used hired killers to run his business. He bribed government officials, contributed to the deterioration of our social structure, and evaded paying taxes. Our leaders, relying on the punishment of lawbreakers to solve the problem of alcohol consumption in America, failed to understand that just making something illegal won't cause it to stop. They eventually realized that it might be easier to bring this problem under control if they began to deal with it more openly and honestly. As a result, it's now legal again to possess and drink alcoholic beverages. People are no longer killed in the trafficking of this substance. There is still the problem of alcohol abuse, of course, but today some employers have rehabilitation programs to help people kick the habit, and there are public service announcements reminding us not to drink and drive. Commercials on television remind us to designate a driver while others drink. Alcoholism is also now recognized as an illness.

We need to find a way to deal with abortion more openly, more effectively, than simply passing laws that make it a hidden and unobservable behavior. If we begin to deal with this problem more openly, even a failure to completely curtail abortion can still result in many successes. I believe this is the way to grow as a people.

Returning to the main subject, abortion --- in the long run, many more lives will be saved if abortion is kept legal and safe. The lives of the unborn are at stake, but so are the lives of the young mothers and their children, who could then have long and happy lives, because unplanned pregnancies will no longer be stigmatized. Pregnancies will be something planned, something wanted.

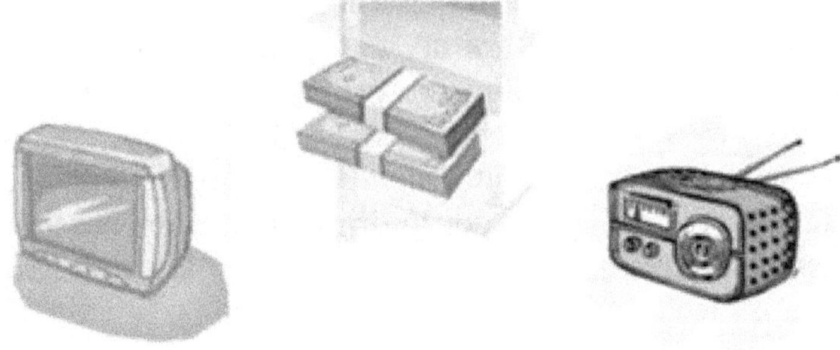

In today's society, television and movies depict virgins as strange, weird people. Promiscuity is portrayed as natural, normal. "Too much honesty" is seen as something only nerds practice. Gunmen get ten times more air time than non-violent characters. Sex and violence pervade the top ten lists in movies, books, television, and video games.

But if you want to train a person to be a priest, you don't take him to a whorehouse for lessons. If you want a boy to become an Eagle Scout, you don't tell him to become a member of a gang. So how can we expect the young people of today to be sexually responsible, given what we feed them on the television and radio?

Section 3: Garbage In, Garbage Out

Some people are surprised at the condition our world is in. The human condition is such a mess. I, on the other hand, am quite surprised that it's not worse. We as a nation consume a terrifying amount of garbage --- the minds of our children are being flooded with sexual misinformation and disinformation. Everywhere we turn, there are sexual messages on TV and radio, on billboards, in news magazines, and pervading the internet. The media inundate us with the sights and sounds of sexual play. It's no wonder our children are so "hot-to-trot."

Let's take a look at what television has been showing us. I didn't really worry about what was on TV until the following occurred --- I received a call from a neighbor, whose daughter had been hurt at school and needed to be taken home for the day. I went to get the child as a favor to my neighbor. When we got back to my apartment, I turned on the TV and asked her what she wanted to watch. She chose a children's channel. We sat and watched for a while, and then something happened that struck me as strange. In the video we saw, a woman was trying to get her husband's attention. He was watching football and she seemed to feel left out. She dangled a pair of panties in front of him to lure him away from the TV set. At this point, I began to realize what our children are facing. Somewhat startled, I asked the young girl, "Is this the children's TV station?" She said, "Yes, sir, this is Nickelodeon," or something like that. I started to change the channel, but then I thought, "If this is the children's channel, who knows what's on the other channels?"

The message I'm trying to get across is that much of the material our children see may lead them to ask questions that shouldn't be answered until much later, or just may encourage them to be sexually active far too early. It's worth noting that there are hardly any programs on TV that encourage children to keep their virginity. Is it any wonder we have teenage pregnancy problems? A young girl raised in this "cherry-popping" environment might find it strange to think that anyone appearing on TV was ever a virgin. On TV, virgins are rarely portrayed as virtuous people. Instead, virgins are usually portrayed as stuck-up, prudish, nerdish, childish misfits. Is it any wonder that girls rush to get their "cherries" taken, almost as if keeping their virginity were some kind of health hazard?

Television is likely one of the most significant contributors to many of the sexual problems we have as a society, but it's far from being the only culprit. Some popular music is just as bad, if not worse. One song I've heard, entitled (approximately) "Walk on the Wild Side," refers to a girl who doesn't lose her cool even when she's giving oral sex. The words "giving head" are quite clear and easy to understand. The song was played regularly on a major radio station throughout the day in a large metropolitan area. How inspiring it must be, when it's heard by our sons and daughters! Another song, entitled (approximately) "Juicy Fruit," was on another well-known radio station. One of the lines went something like this: "I will be your lollipop, you can lick me anywhere." A shorter line in the same song says "You're so juicy." Is it any wonder parents' groups are banding together to make the music industry label albums to indicate mature themes in such songs? No wonder sex education classes in our schools make little impact --- there's not enough positive, useful, accurate, constructive sexual information out there to contend with the billions spent by businesses each year on the most provocative and seductive advertising money can buy. You can't drive down the highway without seeing giant billboards of bikini-clad women, displaying their "assets" for all to see. We, and our children, are being overrun with sexual images. One rap musician referred in one song to a female he desired as being as "soft as a pillow" while he was "as hard as steel." The airwaves are literally being "screwed" up. These things we're all witnessing don't even include the subliminal messages assaulting our subconscious and affecting our behavior.

Perhaps you can now see why I say that we're not aiming at the right target. There might not be so many unwanted pregnancies if sex wasn't used as a tool to get us to purchase goods and services. Our daughters might not be so promiscuous, if they weren't being taught by TV, radio, billboards, etc., that they're supposed to be entertainment for men. What good would it do to outlaw abortion when half the world is screaming to our children to "have sex if you want to be with the 'in' crowd"? It's no wonder children think that all their peers are "doing it." They're too young to realize that **not** everyone is doing it, despite seeing everyone on TV doing it. We put garbage in the minds of our youth; this is the main reason we get garbage out. So the moral of the story is that it's hard to stay clean when you live in a dump. We need to clean up the dump, not cover it up.

The devil is in the doorway. He's opening the door of opportunity. Behind him, in the darkness, loom drug and alcohol abuse, gambling, pornography, theft, murder, and all varieties of sin and crime. The devil is looking for more ways to corrupt our lives and bring us into the darkness. He has people "on standby," waiting to provide illegal abortions. This will help his empire grow, since he knows that he's in charge of abortions, whether they're legal or illegal. He would rather abortion be made illegal, so that no one can know the magnitude of the problem, and so that his government --- and not yours --- will control and manage the practice of abortion.

Section 4: Another Foothold for the Underground

Organized crime --- the underworld, the black market --- is stronger than ever. Illegal abortion helps make the underworld even more powerful. To demonstrate this, I offer a brief report on some of the conditions of our world today, hoping this will lead to a better understanding of the problem. First, let me explain what I mean by "the underworld." Who are these people? The people of the underworld are the ones who control illegal gambling, prostitution, drug use, and trafficking in stolen goods, among other things. To most people, such activities are rare, isolated incidents. For others, this is a way of life.

It's assumed by most people that the police are in control of this situation, but this is debatable. To begin with the drug problem, America has been receiving heroin from the Middle East for decades. Any addict who wants heroin can get it, day or night. Cocaine enters America from South America, and the cocaine traffic is a bloody, risky, multibillion-dollar business. The drug lords of South America have become so rich, so powerful, that they have successfully declared war on the US Department of Justice, and have been actively involved in the murder of at least one American judge. They have infiltrated their own government so thoroughly that they grow thousands of acres of coca plants (the source of cocaine) in the open, and yet are rarely arrested. Many South American and Central American countries are controlled or greatly influenced by these drug lords, and as soon as these criminals can install a president in charge of one of these countries, they can wage war on other nations, be represented in the United Nations as a sovereign country, and use their people's taxes to help grow more drugs and buy better equipment to smuggle drugs. They will also enjoy diplomatic immunity from arrest. They are close to achieving these objectives now, if they haven't already.

Gambling doesn't have a much better reputation. In many places, gambling is now considered respectable. Its illicit and degrading history has been all but forgotten. The gambling lords practically owned Nevada at one time, and many other parts of the world as well. They have become an integral part of the entertainment business in our society. Many people have become hooked on gambling; many have lost their futures, their souls, and their lives --- and no one seems to be shocked or amazed or overly concerned about it.

Smut is also a big money-maker today. All kinds of sexual acts may be bought for a price; sometimes they're free. This part of the underworld was controlled by pimps, until the pornographers got involved, and these people are also beginning to influence our laws. It's no coincidence that in the country that exports the largest amount of child pornography to America, the laws have been changed to make the age of consent for girls 13 years of age. In other words, at an age when most girls have not become physically or mentally mature, 13-year-old girls may consent to have sex when they choose and with whom they choose. I can only assume that pedophiles must be running that country.

In Italy, a pornographic movie actress was a member of parliament for five years, and is now a role model for young Italian girls, as a leader and a lawmaker. Pornography is no longer an underground material. You can find explicit material at any adult bookstore in this country, and there are many such stores. Child pornography (depicting nude children) and "snuff films" (which include genuine death scenes) are currently illegal, but for how long?

All of which brings us to this point --- we really only have two choices when it comes to abortion. We can keep it legal, and easy for the government to monitor, or we can help the underground create a new branch of operations for themselves. Many doctors and medical students already know the procedure for giving an abortion; for them, not giving abortions would mean passing up a small fortune on the side. Many doctors and students have good administrative skills, which means they could easily run a sizable operation of this kind.

If too many doctors and students were to get involved in organized crime, it would only be a matter of time before they employed their business skills to form organized crime syndicates, syndicates with a sophistication never before witnessed. We can limit the growth of organized crime by keeping abortion and other unwanted behaviors legal, legal enough to keep the truly evil element out.

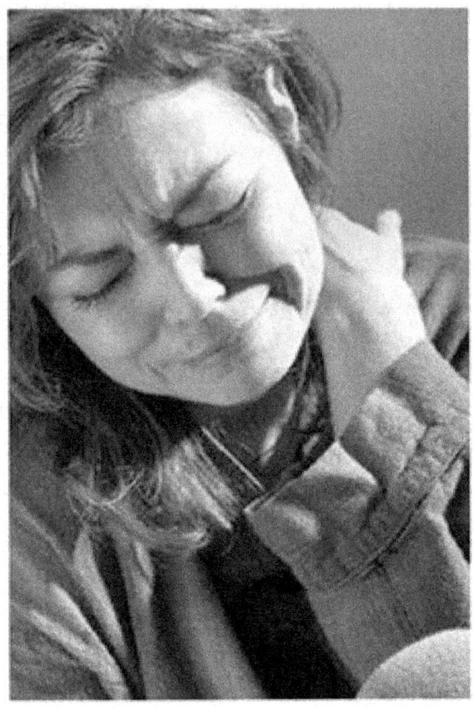

No rapist should have the right to force his victim to bear his child. No woman should have to carry a baby illegally forced upon her. No child should have to be born with a rapist for a father and an abused victim for a mother. God knows this is not right.

Section 5:

Rape

Some people believe that abortion should always be illegal, even for victims of rape. For the most part, men cannot relate to this issue at all. In many parts of America, nearly twenty percent of the female population has been raped at one time or another. Many more women have been victims of sexual harassment or sexual abuse of one kind or another. If this many women have been victims of rape, harassment, or sexual abuse, it stands to reason that there must be a sizable population of rapists and abusers, who have been victimizing the female population. It has been known for some time that women aren't fairly treated by law enforcement officials, nor do they get real justice from the judicial system. Many men still do not consider rape a serious crime. On this issue, men should not be allowed to decide the fate of women.

Whether women should be allowed to abort a fetus that is a result of rape should be entirely up to the female population. This is not just a personal issue for women --- it's also an issue only women can understand. On this particular issue, men should recuse themselves and give women the control and power they need to decide, on their own, what the law should be as it pertains to victims of rape and abortion. As much as men may try to empathize or sympathize with women on this issue, they cannot. No man will ever have to bear a child that is the result of a violent and brutal rape. Men cannot know the humiliation and degradation of being this kind of victim. To be forced to nourish and care for a fetus that you do not want, or will not love, is cruel, oppressive, and obscene.

In looking for a solution to this problem, we can go a long way toward stopping rape by using DNA identification methods, much as we now use fingerprints. Rape is such an intimate crime that a perpetrator can't help leaving traces of his DNA. When we're born, our footprints and fingerprints are taken. We should also keep a sample of blood and a record of our genetic patterns, our DNA. We can uniquely identify anyone through DNA matching, or at least come very close. Therefore, rape should almost always be a solvable crime. A strand of hair or a drop of semen or blood may be all it takes to apprehend these criminals. Women should band together and lobby Congress to require that we store each person's genetic "fingerprint" in a DNA database. This would be useful not only in combating the crime of rape, but any crime. Since we can use DNA to uniquely identify individuals, or come very close, we should, therefore, begin to lay a foundation for such a DNA database by taking blood samples from newborns, starting now. If by doing this we can succeed in reducing the incidence of rape, this will also decrease the occurrence of pregnancies due to rape, and help to diminish the incidence of child abuse and child molestation.

I'd like to make one other suggestion. If we actually outlaw all abortion, even when the pregnancy is a result of rape, this would give new rights to rapists. Any rapist would be able to force a woman he has victimized to bear his child. Such criminals could father as many children as they like, as long as they didn't get caught, because their victims would have no right to abort their fetuses. Further, giving fetuses a right to live also protects rapists who might otherwise propagate their bloodlines through criminal behavior. And if it's true that nearly a fifth of the female population is raped at one point or another, and that our genes do determine to some degree our level of intelligence, or have some influence on the likelihood that we might be a criminal, then outlawing all abortions may give rapists the chance to breed criminals by using unsuspecting women to carry and deliver the criminals of the future.

When legality is for sale to the highest bidder, there can be no justice. When the size of your wallet determines whether you may or may not have a safe and legal abortion, the law is for sale. If people with money can have safe and legal abortions, while the rest cannot, we can no longer call this country a land of "liberty and justice for all." We may have to change that to the land of "liberty and justice for all who can afford it."

Section 6:

Preference to the Rich

Laws should be made with everyone in mind, since "the equal protection of the laws" is one of the cornerstones of the US Constitution. If abortion is made illegal, there cannot be equal treatment under the law, if only because the rich would have an obvious advantage over the poor. We already know that the rich and privileged tend to get richer, while the poor tend to get poorer. But why is this?

The abortion issue could be a contributing factor in this scenario. Let's take a hypothetical situation and explore why the rich (the privileged) might get richer, and the poor become poorer, if abortion were made illegal. Those with money would still be able to go where abortions are safe and legal (Canada or Mexico, for instance), and not have to worry about the dangers of illegal abortion, while those who are poor or just afraid of the dangers of illegal abortion will be left with only one choice --- keeping the baby. Only the poor who feel they must have an abortion, in this scenario, will have to endure the fear and the consequences of unsafe and illegal abortion, regardless of the actual degree of safety and legality.

Abortion will not be as much of a factor in the lives of the rich who feel they must have an abortion, because they can afford to go to where abortion is safe and legal. Because of the risk factor, many more poor women will likely decide to keep their babies. As a result, poor women will have bigger families. And as a consequence of having bigger families, the poor will also have more child-rearing-related bills, a higher cost of living, than the rich, who will be able to keep their families small and thereby keep their cost of living low. A law making abortion illegal would drive many of the poor, who are barely making it now, into poverty and onto welfare. The rich, however, will be left untouched. They will only have to answer to their consciences, and their bank accounts.

This also brings up another point we should address. No one should be above the law, but in this case this is obviously not true. No law should be passed that most of us have to live by but some of us do not. We may as well make separate laws, some for the rich and others for the poor. The rich already have enough privileges that others have no hope of enjoying. The poor already have enough roadblocks in their way, without a new law that applies only to them.

Another problem is that those who decide whether abortion should be legal or illegal are often those who can afford to fly their wives and daughters to places where abortion is safe and legal. In other words, the well off would be passing a law that would have no effect on them. They would be making a law for those who don't get to participate as much in the lawmaking process. Some might even say it's another form of taxation without representation --- the poor paying the consequences for a law passed by the rich and privileged.

Such a law would also work in favor of men and against women. As we know, women are often paid less than men for doing the same job; if a law were passed outlawing abortion, this problem would get worse. To understand how this might happen, let's first examine why women get paid less than men now. One reason is because women get pregnant, which affects the number of days they can be at work. Employers spend millions of dollars training employees, and many of these employers feel that such money spent on women can go to waste if a woman becomes pregnant and decides to stop working. Also, some men are chauvinists who want to "keep women down."

But because women may have to be retrained more often than men (because of leaves of absences due to pregnancies) in order to catch up to where they were before taking leave, some employers use this as an excuse to pay women less than men in general. If abortion were outlawed, this problem would become worse --- if a woman's sexuality can be used against her now, what would happen if a law were passed giving her even less control over her freedom of choice concerning unwanted pregnancies? Would employers consider women less valuable or more valuable? Those who support the women's movement will see that making abortion illegal would restrict women's freedom and their choice of lifestyles.

If abortion were outlawed, it would make an economic difference in women's lives --- a difference in favor of those with more money, and in favor of men. Is there a conspiracy to keep women "barefoot and pregnant"? Are we seeing a re-domestication of women? There are many men trying to make abortion illegal, as soon as possible, even though they will never have to decide whether they themselves should have an abortion. Again, this is mainly a women's issue --- it affects women, and it should be decided by women. If we can get the men, and the rich and privileged, out of the decision-making process concerning this issue, and get more middle-class and lower-middle-class women into the process, a law outlawing abortion might then be supportable (not really!). But until then, "No way, José."

To say it again, this is truly a women's issue, but hardly anyone pays attention to the fact that our House of Representatives and our Senate are predominantly male-controlled institutions. As male-run institutions, they do not and cannot understand this problem. The courts, also mostly men, are also not qualified to decide this issue, for the same reason. When there are as many women on the bench as there are men, then this might be an issue the courts can fairly decide. Until then, the closest this country will ever come to settling this issue fairly would be if we put it to a vote by the general public. We need to petition our lawmakers to put this issue to a public vote so we can settle it. (Remember that there are more women than men.) The politicians have used the abortion problem as a re-election tool for too long --- it's the people (a majority of whom are women) who have to live with this problem, so it's only right that the people (a majority of whom are women) should decide the issue.

We're all different in various ways, and therefore not necessarily physically, mentally, morally, or socio-economically equal, but we're supposed to be legally equal, equal under the law. We should, therefore, share the legal responsibility of abortions. The right-to-lifers are trying to outlaw abortion, but men cannot be left out of the equation, because they are full partners in conception. As such, we should consider a new law, just for men --- if a fetus is to be aborted, the father must pay the mother half of what his child support payments would have been, for nine years. Why? Let's call it **abortion support**. If we really want to stop abortions, we should try that! It's easy (for men) if only women have to bear the brunt of the shame and fear that go along with having an abortion; let's share the problem and then see how willing men are to make unwanted babies.

This, of course, is "see no evil, speak no evil, hear no evil."

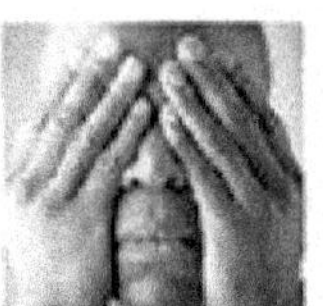  

Let's face it. This is why we live in such a screwed up world. We're all like these three. We don't hear what we don't want to hear, we won't look at what we should see, and we won't say what we should say. If our aim as a people were the pursuit of truth, our children would be raised right and abortion would be only an insignificant occurrence. This image also depicts the religious conservative movement --- the people who would rather hide the abortion problem behind the law than see it for what it is, who try not to listen to what they must hear to make things right, who avoid speaking out against the things that enable it.

Section 7:
Lost Souls

An even more important issue is that there's a continuous struggle going on, a struggle between good and evil. In this daily struggle, souls are won and lost on both sides. The victor in this struggle will be determined by the people, because we are beings of superior, free will. We humans are the dominant creatures of this world. The fight for souls is fought on the battleground of moral issues; on this battleground, we must all choose sides on each moral issue in our lives. In this section, we'll explore one view of this struggle.

For the sake of argument, let's say that at this time neither good nor evil has completely taken over yet. Both good and evil are weakened by battle, both have sustained damage to their defenses. Law and order, God and the church, are fighting for good. Organized crime, greed, and the devil are working on behalf of evil. But it may be that the good intentions of the pro-life movement may lead to more evil than good. This is what I fear will happen if the courts decide to outlaw abortion. Most pro-lifers believe that abortion is wrong, and therefore want to outlaw it, but I feel that there's nothing the devil would like more than to see abortion outlawed --- it would then be easier to win souls to the dark side. The government would no longer know how many abortions are being performed, and would no longer know whether the rate of unwanted pregnancies is getting better or worse.

There are a few worst-case scenarios we need to examine before a good decision can be made on this issue. For one, yet another segment of society would be lost to organized crime. We know from our experience with drugs that wherever there is a need, it will be met, whether the service is legal or not. If we outlaw abortion, we'll be giving organized crime a chance to expand its already vast empire of graft and corruption. Organized crime would also have the chance to influence people who, up until now, have made only one serious mistake (becoming pregnant by accident, or as a result of coercion). Let's say that a young mother-to-be is aware of, or has been told about, an underground operation that could and would perform an abortion for her. What if the underground abortionist used the opportunity to give this mother-to-be a drug (to control the pain) that was very habit-forming? By the time she was past the immediate effects of the abortion, she might be hooked on the pain-killing drugs given her by the abortionist. Now we have a person who has inadvertently become hooked on drugs.

A drug addict is as good a slave as organized crime can hope for; the crime lords know that if they can get drugs to people, they'll create for themselves a slave population that will lie, cheat, steal, prostitute themselves, and even kill to get those drugs. Some young women, trying to erase the mistake of an unwanted pregnancy, end up as drug-abusing prostitutes. This makes organized crime stronger, and helps crime grow faster, along with AIDS and the continued destruction of the American family.

Making abortion illegal will not make it go away, despite what the pro-lifers apparently believe. Again, if abortion is outlawed, we may never know with any certainty how many unwanted pregnancies actually occur --- the only reason we know now is because abortion is dealt with openly and legally. As long as it's legal, we can know the magnitude of the situation, attack the true problem (unwanted pregnancies), and one day overcome it. If abortion were outlawed, no one who intended to have an abortion would ever admit to being pregnant, and we as a society would remain ignorant of the problem, and likely pretend it has gone away. A new drain on the American economy could begin --- women would spend money not only on illegal abortions in the US, but also in Canadian and Mexican hospitals. I'm sure you see the picture now --- there are many ways to get around such a law, no matter how well intended its purpose.

Of course, the worst-case scenario is where a pregnant woman seeks an illegal abortion (assuming abortion is outlawed), and is killed by an abortion provider who lacked proper tools or training. There may be a great deal of truth to the saying that it's darkest before the dawn. When abortion was illegal in this country, most people were fairly satisfied with the situation, until the deaths of some young and otherwise good girls showed us how ugly our society, and our toothless laws, had become. Abortion was made legal to put an end to this ugliness, and for the first time we began to keep records and discovered how extensive the problem was.

But now we have a new ugliness to resolve, the fact that our society is sexually out of control, and far too many unwanted pregnancies are occurring. We've tried sex education, only to find that it has not yet been overly effective in helping to prevent unwanted pregnancy. Now it seems that we're giving up, because we haven't found a way to stop unwanted pregnancies, and we're back where we started, reconsidering the old solution of outlawing abortion. Doing so would not benefit God, the church, or the general law and order of our society. We **could** all pretend that the problem has gone away, and childishly sweep the problem under the rug. But this is not a real solution, of course.

Let's deal with this new era of sexual openness in our society. We can find answers that will make abortions a thing of the past, when we've learned to deal with and control our sexual nature. Some people have learned how to control their sexual nature; it's just a matter of finding out what they know. I believe this problem can be solved, and if our government won't do what it takes, we need to get our churches, sororities, fraternities, PTAs, and whomever else we can get, to lend a helping hand. So far, it looks as if the sad but honest truth is that we've become too comfortable with our promiscuous and irresponsible lifestyle --- many souls have already been lost to lustful, lewd, lascivious behavior. The key to our situation may be the behavior of each and every one of us, not just the few who took a chance and lost (became pregnant). It may well be that our so-called adults will need to be educated, more so than the children, since there surely are no easy answers to this problem. Maybe we should teach adults what should and shouldn't be allowed on TV, what should or shouldn't be allowed on the radio, on billboards, and so forth.

Ms. Liberty can accomplish much, but there are limits to even her power. We too often depend on external powers --- we look to God, we look to the law. Sometimes the answer can be found there, but sometimes the answer is within us. We must turn our minds, hearts, and souls in the same direction, so that outside help (except for God's help) is not required. We must be of one mind, one heart, and one soul.

Section 8:

Right or

Wrong May

Not be the Issue

It is simple-minded at best to say to ourselves that abortion is always right or always wrong. It's quite possible that it is neither. This overly simplistic approach has been taken by right-to-lifers (the Moral Majority), who have completely ignored the fact that no one "enjoys" having an abortion. These people would have us believe that there's some kind of huge "abortion party" going on, and that they, at least, are "too moral" to join in the festivities. They have ignored the fact that everyone knows (deep down inside) that abortion is wrong, and that some women have simply gotten lost in the shuffle of a mismanaged society, and felt they had no other option. These people (the Moral Majority / right-to-lifers) have invoked God and religion to run roughshod over lost, hurt women with their self-righteousness. The law God has given us (the commandment "Thou shalt not kill") is a just and good law, but we live in a world where people are frequently killed in the name of the Lord.

We should all be aware that the issue is not as simple as right or wrong. These women are not **trying** to get pregnant, just so they can run down to the nearest abortion clinic for the "pleasure" of having an abortion. Slapping them with a new law making abortion illegal would only make matters worse. In this section, I'd like to look at this issue from another point of view, so I'll present circumstances that will hopefully help us all understand why some women do have abortions.

Fear often plays a major role in the decision-making process. As we know, there has not been and there is not now a national consensus, or even an awareness, in many cases, of how the topic of sex should be handled in the home. In our culture, sex is often still taboo. Parents are left to make their own decisions as to how they'll handle the topic of sex in their households. As we might expect in such a case, the methods used to deal with the issue of sex are quite varied. One of the many methods used to discourage our youth from having sex is to threaten them. Such threats are often all too believable to the young people involved --- in some homes, the male authority figure is physically abusive, and may beat the children and/or the mother of the children. Many young girls fear that they'll be severely beaten if it's discovered that they've been sexually active. They fear being beaten because they've been told they'll be beaten if it's discovered that they've been sexually active. They believe it because, often, they've been beaten for lesser "transgressions." No law making abortion illegal can mean much to a girl who fears being beaten. The only choice such girls see is between having an abortion and getting beaten senseless, likely ending up in the hospital, or worse. Anyone threatened with such a beating is likely to worry more about that than about any government-made law.

Even though the true figures on child abuse aren't known for certain, it's a fact that the problem is more widespread than most observers have expected. However, something much less dreadful than a direct threat to her physical safety can cause a girl to seek an abortion --- many girls are told that if they become pregnant, they must leave home. This may not be the worst prospect for some, but to others who live in otherwise nice homes, this can be a very frightening thought. The fear of living in a slum area on welfare, or in a high-crime area, away from the people they love, is enough to make many girls seek abortions. The thought that they might have to live in a place they wouldn't even want to visit is enough to send many girls running, full speed, to the nearest abortion clinic. The above reasons obtain more often than most people think.

But it's not always a case of a threat to one's health or the possible loss of one's home. In a very close family, just the shame and humiliation of being discovered to be pregnant, and labeled a tramp, can drive a young woman to the nearest clinic. Some might say that if she had just kept her legs closed, she wouldn't be in such a predicament. If this is how you feel, you should know you're a part of the problem, not the solution. Most girls who become pregnant find themselves in that situation not because they want to break the law, but because of misinformation they've received, or a lack of information about love and sex, and the consequences of being sexually active. These are often lost, misinformed young girls, not criminals. They're young people whose hormones are often working overtime, making them physically and sexually mature, and the fact is that, for a time, our sex drives seem to be more powerful than our brains. This happens to just about everyone. Almost no one goes through life without taking a chance with unprotected sex; some are simply luckier than others.

Until we as a nation begin to create some kind of comprehensive plan, by which the youth of our culture are guided slowly and steadily into mature adulthood, we'll continue to have the same problem with the issue of abortion. Most of us will become parents, but our homes and our schools don't teach us to be the parents we will most likely become. If we're ever to resolve this issue, we'll have to stop focusing on abortion itself, and focus instead on training, for all, in Planned Parenthood and child-rearing. I don't have all the answers, but I'm sure that if we put our minds to it, we can surely find better answers than the ones we have now. Right or wrong, black or white, good or evil . . . it's just not that simple. We have a long way to go as a civilization, and we'll solve this problem one day. But it will not be the law that saves us from our predicament.

I am sure, however, that America will find the answer. It's more likely that we will find the answer than it is that any other country will. If you've seen TV in other parts of the world, you've noticed that they're much more decadent and openly sexual in their media, and in their lifestyles. America, on its own terms, is more conservative and religious than most of the rest of the world. For whatever reason, we've been blessed, and, just as the women's movement matured here, so civil and human rights have grown faster here than almost anywhere else. As world leaders in this regard, we must take the next step and show the world that mankind can actually grow above and beyond our laws. We've done it with respect to group, racial, and social issues; now we must build a society that will allow us to mature psychologically, and heal ourselves individually.

It's easy to say abortion is either right or wrong, but if you read your Bible, you'll realize that very often it's hard to know which is the right way and which is the wrong way. Even the kings in the Bible asked the prophets which way was right, and Jesus would sometimes correct the Apostles because they didn't always know the right way. One man addressed Jesus as "My good man," and Jesus said: "Only the Father (God) is good." He didn't even include himself in the category of "good." We, therefore, shouldn't pretend that we're anything other than sinners, and it's not a sinner's place to judge others.

Brain fart.
This is a Christian on self-righteousness.

Don't get me wrong. I'm no angel, not by a long shot. As we're taught, we're all sinners. However, some of us can see what's wrong with everyone else, but not what's wrong with ourselves. We don't recognize that that's a sin. If you can see the small blemishes of others, but can't see the large blemishes of your own, that's a "brain fart," something the conservative right is all too good at. That's not the only brain fart, though --- when you've fixed yourself, you may then fix others. Until then, do us all a favor and shut up.

Section 9:

From Pro-Choice

to No Choice

We stand at the edge of a precipice. Progressives in America are seemingly losing ground (at the Supreme Court) to an ever more regressive, intolerant, conservative right. In 2005 and 2006, two new, young Supreme Court Justices, Roberts and Alito, were appointed. With one or two more conservative Supreme Court Justices, *Roe v. Wade* could be overturned, and it may again become illegal to have an abortion in the United States. Women's rights will diminish. Many women will be saddled with children they'll be forced to bear, even when their pregnancies were a result of rape or molestation. Such a new law would, effectively, answer such women as if someone had said, "Oh well, I guess you're stuck with it." Back-alley abortions, unqualified abortionists, women showing up in emergency rooms because of botched abortions, and a rise in suicides because of the additional stress of abortion's illegality, will all increase significantly, and all so that the Moral Majority can feel self-righteously good.

Democrats and liberals, fasten your seat belts, because we're in for a rough ride. For this travesty of justice to be averted, we'll need Democrats in the White House until the Supreme Court can be rebalanced, and at least two conservative Justices have been replaced with more reasonable judges. Some Progressives seem to have very short memories --- few of us remember the real-life nightmare some women suffered before *Roe v. Wade*. At that time, if a woman was raped or molested, and she became pregnant as a result, aborting that fetus made her a criminal. These women had to go underground, sometimes to very unsavory characters, seeking illegal abortions from back-alley abortionists. There was no oversight or government regulation to protect them. They had no legal choice in the matter. In my opinion, it would be a lapse in judgment to turn back the hands of time and make abortion illegal once more.

The religious right, conservative Christians, Moral Majority, Bible-thumpers, or whatever we should call them, have already made their judgment; they're the force behind Republicans appointing judges who will do their bidding. But who are they to judge? They believe they're godly people, but **what does God say about people who judge others? My Bible study regarding people judging others yielded interesting results.** It made me wonder if these conservative Christians read the Bible. At the very least, they might want to look a little deeper into their Bibles, because I don't think they've read what I found: at the risk of coming across as a preacher, I encourage you to read the following Bible passages (or just keep reading).

Romans 14:13 --- Let us not, therefore, judge one another: But judge this rather that no man put a stumbling block or an occasion to fall in his brother's (sister's) way.

Or maybe this passage:

James 4:12 --- There is one lawgiver (God), who is able to save and to destroy: Who art thou that judgest another?

Or maybe this passage, in the words of Jesus:

Luke 6:37 --- Judge not, and ye shall not be judged: condemn not, and ye shall not be condemned: forgive and Ye shall be forgiven.

Or this:

John 7:24 --- Judge not according to the appearances, but judge righteous judgment.
Or maybe this:

Romans 2:1 --- Therefore thou art inexcusable, O man, whosoever thou art that judgest: For wherein thou judgest another, thou condemnest thyself; for thou that judgest doest the same things.
Or this:

James 4:11 --- Speak not evil of one another, Brethren (sisters). He (she) that speaketh evil of his brethren (sisters) and judgeth his brethren (sisters), speaks evil of the law.
And one last quote on judging others, one I think we all know, one spoken by Jesus:

John 8:7 --- He that is without sin among you, let him (her) first cast a stone at her.

To end this section with a lesson from God, too many so-called Christians believe that all that matters is the innocence of the child, or the life of the child. But the Bible shows us this is not so. God himself killed a newborn baby, because it was the product of crime and sin. In the story of David, we learn that King David saw Bathsheba and desired her. After she became pregnant by David, David had her husband killed and married Bathsheba. In the second book of Samuel (2 Samuel 12:15), we read: “And the Lord struck the child that Uriah’s wife bare for David, and it was very sick.” In 2 Samuel 12:18: “And it came to pass on the seventh day, the child died.” But the child was a product of King David’s crime and sin. The child did nothing wrong!

It’s not **people** we need to fix, but the system under which we, the people, live. We live in a nation almost entirely geared to the advantage and convenience of corporate employers. This system often requires that we leave our children with strangers, or leave them unattended. Mothers and fathers work such long hours that they effectively leave their children parentless. One reason our teenagers too often wander into the arms of pedophiles and abusers is because normal, regular jobs, held by husbands and fathers, are often no longer sufficient to support their families and allow the mothers to stay home with the children, letting them all live the American dream.

It’s been estimated that one in twenty men is a pedophile. If this is true, there are about 7,500,000 pedophiles out there, in the malls with your children, and walking your neighborhoods, looking for latchkey children at home alone. The money-grubbing system we all live under helped bring this situation about. We live in an environment that makes unwanted pregnancies much more likely. And we mustn’t forget date rape and all the other ways unplanned pregnancies are brought about, ways beyond what most of us can imagine. If conservative Christians have their way, all the women and girls who have become victims of such circumstances could also be made criminals.

Choice is God-given.

In the Book of Revelation, the Bible teaches that on the Day of Judgment, the Book of Life will be opened, and we will be judged by our works. I believe that our "works" are the choices we make throughout our lives. God gives us examples of when we may rightly judge other men and women, but the rest of the choices we make should be only between ourselves and God.

Adam and Eve were placed in Paradise, and given the "choice" between life and death. God said "Of all the trees in the Garden, do not eat from the Tree of the Knowledge of Good and Evil."

We failed to obey God in this, and he has not judged us yet!

But he gave us choice.

Section 10:

More Brain Fart

In this section, I address those so-called Christians who vehemently support the "right-to-life" movement. They may not read this section, and even if they do, they may tear it out and use it as toilet paper. But if they do read this section in its entirety, they'll at least learn that pro-choice people can be just as human --- and just as godly --- as they. We too are God's children.

Let me remind you once again that I may repeat myself, by way of reinforcing an idea.

First, we're **all** pro-life, even those who call themselves pro-choice. We **all** (not just they) believe that children are precious. And not a single soul looks forward to having an abortion.

Having said this, let's deal further with the "brain fart." Those who would outlaw all abortion often vilify young women who have been raped, molested, coerced, blackmailed, extorted, or sexually abused, all to justify their wrongful self-righteousness. They would make such women endure a life of mental and socio-economic imprisonment with the law they want passed, the law that would make abortion illegal. They forget that they're no better than these women. They try to forget that some of their own sisters, daughters, wives, and mothers have also had abortions. They oversimplify God's word by calling abortion murder, while paying billions in taxes to a government responsible for the destruction of thousands of lives --- and call it patriotism. They pay for the killing of walking, breathing souls, **in faraway lands**, for their own protection, but would refuse those who have been forced into pregnancy the right to take their lives back. If God himself destroyed the life of an innocent child because it was conceived in crime and sin, then who are they to make a woman keep a baby conceived in crime and sin? These abused and battered women are not less Christian, less human, or less worthy than others. They're simply less fortunate.

These people call themselves Christians, but their judgment in such cases is completely godless. I say this because I had the same godless, judgmental attitude before God found me. I said things such as "Look at those Christians. They lie, they steal, they cheat, they kill, and then on Sunday, they go to church." If we read the Bible, we see that God tell us which things we're authorized to judge. He gives examples of what kinds of thieves we may judge, and what kinds of killers we may judge; abortion is **not** on the list of things we may judge. Why isn't it on the list, when God himself has killed an innocent child?

Our high rate of abortion is a sign of the End Times. It's a sign that the structure of our families has fragmented, has disintegrated to the point where we simply no longer know with any reasonable degree of certainty who is "screwing" whom. This is the real problem, this is what we must overcome! Our children are scattered by divorce, and lack their parents' interest. Our employers have more influence over us than our families do. The people we do business with rape our finances, diluting our worth, to the point where men often cannot support their families without the assistance of their wives.

Just for a moment, let's take a quick look at an instructive example right here in today's society. I'd be willing to bet that there are very few (if any) incidents of abortion among the Amish. They refuse to live the helter-skelter lifestyles we follow: they know where their children are, and they know where each other is, for such a large portion of their lives, that they have a higher degree of certainty regarding almost all such things. I'd also be willing to bet that their divorce rate is much lower than that of society in general, and the incidence of homosexuality and lesbianism is also much lower. The incidence of violence in school, and problems with dysfunctional children, is lower. They live closer to the land and closer to God, and they have a much lower rate of such problems. I know we're not all going to join the Amish; many of us don't even want to become godly. But our culture has become so full of such problems that it's destroying our family structure, and we must address these problems with our way of life to fix this issue. When we have a godly world, unwanted pregnancies will be a thing of the past, and certainly pregnancies will not be brought about by force. The high incidence of unwanted pregnancies today is a symptom of a greater problem --- an out-of-control social structure --- or, in our case, the lack of a proper social structure.

I am aware, and have not forgotten, that some simple-minded people respect nothing. Some of these people become pregnant, and have abortions. Why should we further punish such children, children who will have such people for mothers? I know where these souls go when they're cut short of a whole life --- straight to heaven. We must let God be the judge of these mothers. Let us, as Christians, make the world into a family-friendly place, where abortions, robberies, murders, and fraud are almost nonexistent. Until we do, evil will continue to flourish, regardless of whether a specific form of evil happens to be legal or illegal.

I'm going to make three rather bold statements, and then I'll explain why they're true. Those who don't understand that making abortion illegal is wrong, after reading these statements and explanations, are, in my opinion, truly blinded by their own self-righteousness.

The devil would support a law making abortion illegal.

Making abortion illegal would lead to worse crime.

Criminals, abusers, and genetic defectives would love a new law making abortion illegal.

Some readers may be asking themselves why the devil would support such a law. It's simple --- the devil knows that laws don't make people behave as they should. He breaks God's laws all the time. He knows that everything deemed illegal falls under his jurisdiction, and lawbreakers will come more completely under his influence. He knows too that making abortion illegal will help the underworld, the black market, organized crime --- or whatever we call it --- grow in influence and power. There will be more dirty money, and more dead mothers, more dead children. He knows that many women, fearing a law making abortion illegal, will keep their babies and raise them, even though these children will grow up unwanted, rejected, and despised --- the perfect conditions to foster future criminals. Yes, the devil would support a law making abortion illegal, just as he revels in the thought of more prisons full of people who felt they had to turn to crime because their country makes no jobs for them.

Next, how will making abortion illegal lead to greater crime? Let me make this next statement stand out, so it can be seen clearly. **If abortion is outlawed, rapists and child molesters would gain the legal right to force women to bear their children. Any freak who could trick a child into sex could not legally be prevented from becoming a father, and any man who raped, extorted, or blackmailed a woman into sex could, under such a law, make the woman keep her unwanted baby. This is beyond criminal. This is the real reason abortion must remain legal.** Pro-lifers, to be honest, should just tell child molesters and rapists: "If you can knock them up, we'll make them have the babies"? **There must not be a law that gives rapists and their kind the legally enforceable right to fatherhood!**

Criminals and genetic misfits would also welcome a law making abortion illegal. The truth is that some men don't become part of the gene pool because they're never chosen by a mate. Unfortunately, this is the natural order of things, part of the Darwinian nightmare of our existence. But if the law were on their side, in their eyes, some would be tempted to take whatever measures they deemed necessary to fulfill their desire to have children, even if doing so landed them in jail, even if they cannot be real fathers to their children.

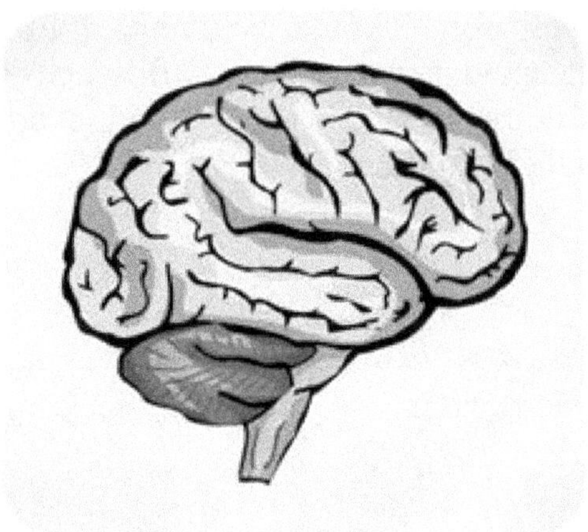

This is "where it is." This is where all answers are understood. This is where we can also find the right questions to ask. The answers are not to be found in our police stations, or in the halls of Congress. And until we begin to develop that very important organ inside our heads, we will flounder in a world of uncertainty.

Section 11:

Our Mentality

I think it's time we take a good look at ourselves. What kind of creatures are we humans? After taking a good look at ourselves, we might not be so surprised at what we've come to be. Some people are appalled at man's inhumanity to himself; perhaps such people never took a good look at the world, perhaps they've lived their lives with their heads buried in the sand. I don't know. But I do know we humans have the potential for such greatness that it staggers the imagination. Our reality, however, is all too often a sad, wretched experience. It often seems as if we're mounting an all-out attack on health and righteousness. How can we be capable of such good, and turn out to be just the opposite? How have we come to the point where we abort thousands of fetuses weekly? When will the greatness we have in our hearts be realized by the actions we take in our daily lives? What kind of animals are we? Let's take that good, hard look at ourselves.

To begin with, let's look at China. In 1989 (it has been said), 2,600 students were killed by government troops for protesting in favor of a more democratic society. The Chinese government, it is suspected, has engaged in the institutionalized murder of thousands, and if all goes according to their plans, this incident will be treated as if it never happened; this was, indeed, their official answer to world inquiries into the matter. In other parts of the world, governments collectively spend billions of dollars to spy on one another, telling their respective peoples that this will make them more secure. America, China, and the Soviet Union have manufactured enough nuclear bombs to destroy the world many times over. And they tell us this makes us safer. Yet none of them have spent half as much on a device that will save our world just once.

Mankind is almost certainly going through a kind of puberty. Like teenagers, we're responsible only when we have to be. We use force as a first resort, instead of a last resort. We manage our world according to whatever the latest crisis happens to be. Short-term goals are given more importance than long-term goals. Yes, it's true. The human race suffers from classic symptoms of adolescence. The good news is that we're better than we used to be. In our childhood, we actually thought that death in battle was an honorable thing. Now it's considered wasteful, for the most part. In our childhood, slavery was considered acceptable, even desirable. The buying and selling of people was even supported by some churches. The North American Indians were nearly wiped out by the incoming Europeans. At the close of our collective childhood, the world sat back and watched the murder of six million Jews by a self-proclaimed Christian named Hitler.

We should try to keep in mind that puberty (or adolescence) might be a critical, and possibly self-destructive, phase of our development. And mankind is on the brink of self-destruction today. History is replete with facts showing that, up until now, mankind has made no real effort to curb his tendency to engage in bloodshed. We have often been no more than murderous, thieving, lying animals, as corrupt as any on this earth. It even seems that we're proud of our sleazy nature. It doesn't seem to be enough that mankind has not gone one day without someone killed by war or crime.

We present as much death and destruction on television as we can. Most of us know at least one person who has been to war; many of us know someone who has killed another human being. We're truly more death-conscious than life-conscious. We still have much of the mentality of a carnivorous beast. We must grow up as a race, as a species. We must leave our self-destructiveness behind, and grow into adulthood before it's too late. Take a good look at the past. Think over the problems we're having with the abortion issue today. Now be truthful. What do you expect of a species that participates in the wholesale destruction of living, breathing adults? What do you expect of a species that has enslaved each other for financial gain? What do you expect of a species that has lynched people, and burned them at the stake? What do you expect of a species that kills in the name of God? What do you expect of a people that destroys the very environment it depends on for survival? What do you expect of a people that watches killing (on television) for entertainment? What do you expect of a race that would stand by and see a person killed in the street, and not even call the police?

What do you expect?

The only reason we have so many strange, destructive things in our lives, things like abortion, is because we've never given children the respect they deserve. It's much easier to rear a child well than to repair an adult. One way to bring our savage lifestyle under control is to raise our children into healthy, responsible adults.

Section 12: Children are more at Risk

One way we could address these problems is to start at the beginning of the life cycle. We need a national policy for rearing children into healthy, responsible adults. We have policies for our national security, for delivering the mail, and for collecting taxes, but we don't have a national policy for how to create a healthy adult. However such a policy might develop, it must start in childhood, for childhood is the foundation of our lives. Our children are not only at risk of being aborted, but also at risk of being slowly murdered after birth. This seems to be a part of the problem that has been ignored. If we continue to destroy the lives of the children who are born, through neglect, they won't value life in their adulthood. They'll be prone to mismanage their lives in such a way as to perpetuate the mistakes their parents made, and the incidence of abortion may never decline.

We have concentrated on abortion, when we should pay more attention to the children who are actually born. In the twenty-first century, children have been driven into a lake and drowned, or dropped out of a window or off a bridge. So many newborns begin life seen as problems, rather than the jewels they are. Too many infants are physically, sexually, and psychologically abused from the day they are born. As a people, we need to structure our lives from beginning to end. We must not continue this free-for-all of madness we call our life cycle. We cannot create the type of atmosphere that will free us from abortion when our entire lives are a crapshoot.

As a people, we know our basic needs are food, clothing, and shelter. As Christians, we know we should obey the Ten Commandments. We know we must behave in a certain way in public. But when will we learn the five most important things to develop our babies' minds? When will the training of our adolescents make them sexually responsible and free of the problem of unwanted pregnancies? When will there be thorough, complete criteria regarding how to be a good parent? Until these kinds of things come to pass, unwanted children will be part of our lives. We have gotten caught up in a vicious cycle. We need healthy-minded adults to break the cycle. But first, we must raise our children right in order to create these healthy-minded adults. When we break this cycle, with a clear-cut and workable plan, violent crime, rape, murder, thievery, and abortion will all begin to diminish. The children of today are exposed to all the worst things life has to offer. This must stop. Crime, racism, sexism, greed, and corruption all come from the same well, the well of general disrespect for life and a loss of godliness.

Jesus loves children so much because he knows that they are our future. He knows God brought them here in the right frame of mind. The answer is not simply getting children into the world, but knowing what to do with them when they get here. Even if we could make every expectant mother have her child, what good is it if they raise murderers, rapists, racists, and thieves? Even life can be a tool for evil, in the wrong hands.

It's nice to imagine that the law can save us from ourselves, but it can't. It's tempting to believe that the law will solve our problems, but it won't. When the Supreme Court is hand-picked with a certain law in mind (reversing Roe v. Wade), how can our Justices be impartial? How can they be just? Maybe that's why Justice is so often depicted blindfolded. She has a sword ready, but will she strike down injustice, or justice?

Section 13: What's the Difference?

There's another question we should ponder: what difference does it make whether a person has an abortion or not? I'm not asking if it makes a difference legally or morally, but what impact does it have on the incidence --- the number of women who have abortions --- whether abortion is legal or illegal? In a study done by Gilda Sedgh of the Guttmacher Institute in the US, along with colleagues from the World Health Organization, it was stated that women are as likely to get abortions in countries where it's outlawed as they are in countries where it's legal. If this is anywhere close to true, it means that making abortion illegal would only make pro-lifers feel as if they accomplished some good. It would be a law with no teeth, a paper tiger. So, if abortions are inevitable regardless of their legality, what "good" thing can we do to make a difference?

There are even more interesting statistics in this study. It states that about 13 percent of maternity mortality (mothers dying with child) worldwide is a result of abortion. Around 70,000 women die annually due to unsafe abortions; around five million suffer permanent or temporary injury. The vast majority of these deaths occur where abortion is illegal. Many children become orphans, and husbands become widowers, when abortion is illegal. Those who call themselves pro-life should consider the lives of the mothers, their other children, and their husbands. The fetuses' lives are not the only ones destroyed by illegal abortion.

I gave an example earlier of how God killed a child because the child was a result of crime and sin. In closing this section, let me cite some of the words of Jesus, and how he felt about children who come from such evil. Children themselves, mind you, are not evil.

Revelation 2:21–23 --- And I gave her space to repent from her fornication; and she repented not. Behold, I will cast her into a bed, and them that commit adultery with her into great tribulation, except they repent of their deeds. **And I will kill her children with death.**

Some say this has nothing to do with abortion, but consider this: what can we call it when the decision to destroy a child has already been made, before the child is ever born? Just as in the case of King David, the children in the above passage are a result of fornication. It could be said that God doesn't like children who are a product of fornication (extramarital sex). Of course he doesn't think all children born as a result of fornication should be killed, but he obviously does make exceptions!

Crack baby epidemic

Fetal alcohol syndrome destroys the unborn

Kiddy- porn found on the internet

Of all the problems in the sewer of our civilization, one is particularly gruesome. Some girls and women are so messed up that they don't have the foggiest notion of how to respect life, whether born or unborn. But they know something the right-to-lifers can't accept --- they are going to destroy their children, one way or another. Some future mothers are on a path so destructive that everything they touch is hurt. They know that nothing can be safe with them, or in their environment. Too many of the unborn are already condemned to a sentence of death, after they're born. We must stay out of it; if we interfere, we may only succeed in extending such children's misery. There are mothers who should not be allowed to raise snakes, let alone children.

Section 14: What about the Rest of this Mess?

The abortion issue turns out to be a politician's dream, because, compared to many other problems, it's easy to politicize. And while we're preoccupied with abortion, what's being done about the rest of the mess we call our world? If abortion is seen as a problem, perhaps we should think about the difficulty of raising a child in today's world. It has been said that the 1980s was a boom time for business. However, three million people were homeless in America (the biggest economy on earth) at this time. Yes, people are living, and dying, in the streets of America. As of March 2010, America was the only first-world nation with no national health plan. AIDS is spreading into our communities. American businessmen are destroying the American economy.

The welfare system was constructed so that it trapped people on welfare instead of helping them return to the workforce. Let's look deeper into the mess. Fifty-one Colombian judges have been killed in the war on drugs. The drug pushers are winning the war on drugs in Colombia. Maybe it's not such a good idea to bring a child into the world. Those who were abused as children should be warned that victims of child abuse are themselves very likely to abuse children. Eighty percent of the prisoners in America were abused and battered as children, or are abusive adults. People who have been abused as children might be better off having abortions if they wish (unless we're prepared to take care of such children). Allowing people who were sexually abused as children to have children of their own could mean a life of misery for their newborns. When people don't want their children, and can't live with giving their children away, we might be wiser to refrain, to not pretend that we know what's best for such people. We may know what's best for ourselves, but without living other people's lives, we shouldn't be so sure we know what's good for them.

As hard as it is to believe, there are people so sick that they actually try to get women pregnant specifically so they can have their own children to molest. In doing so, they don't run the risk that the children will inform their parents of the abuse. Some young girls know that their parents aren't fit to raise children, and they'd rather abort their children than allow them to grow up as playthings for damaged adults, adults who would be quite willing to destroy innocent childhoods just to satisfy their lewd and lascivious needs.

We also can't forget that abortion isn't always just the fault of the mothers; very often the society we live in creates the need for abortions. We live in a society where our employers can move us without any notice at all. This can leave people bankrupt, or financially distressed. Some become homeless. As Americans, we can expect to be left "out in the cold" by our employers several times over the course our careers. There are even occasions where pregnant mothers lose their jobs, and there will always be those who won't bring a child into the world in such circumstances. Corporate instability is the cause of many hardships in America, and it's one reason abortion is still with us. Some people feel they already have enough problems on their hands; if their world and their personal lives are already a mess, they often wonder why they should contribute to making life worse for everyone, especially children.

Our society has a kind of tunnel vision when it comes to social causes. We need to pay attention to the problem at hand, but also to the rest of the mess. There are many reasons women seek abortions, so many that it's sometimes impossible for anyone to make a good decision, and all the more so for the women in that position. Let's briefly revisit why abortions are inevitable, and then we'll look at some less common reasons why abortion won't simply come to an end.

Right-to-lifers are fond of using the rationale that a woman can always give a baby up for adoption, if needed. They forget, or just refuse to realize, that it's not just pregnancy that these young women fear --- they often fear being found out by others, such as their parents. As mentioned earlier, some young girls face being thrown out of their homes, if they're found to be pregnant. Some know they would be severely beaten or otherwise abused if found out. Girls in these situations often feel that they can't simply put their babies up for adoption. For them, being pregnant, or even just being sexually active, may cause them to lose something they can't replace, or may so damage their physical or mental well being that they fear for their lives.

However, there are other, stranger reasons women seek abortions. Some parents may simply be ignorant when it comes to how to use birth control properly. Some couples are simply swept away in the throes of passion, and apparently become temporarily insane. But often the reasons are too personal for them to explain to others; these more personal reasons are the topic of this section.

We can start with cases of incest, because there are girls who are victims of incestuous relationships. Some fathers, mothers, uncles, stepfathers, and other relations sexually abuse younger members of the family. A victim of this kind of abuse may realize that when her child is born, there's a significant risk that her baby will also be abused by that same parent or relation. Some young girls, with nowhere else to go, may seek abortions because they're trying to save their babies from what they feel is a fate worse than death --- a life of abuse. Prostitutes who become pregnant may fear that their pimps might want to use their children in child pornography, or sell them to pedophiles (children are still being sold into slavery today). It's not hard to understand why a woman might want an abortion under such circumstances. The realization that her child might be used as a slave, or wind up in the hands of people who might kill or experiment on the child, may be too much to bear for a mother-to-be. Drug-addicted mothers will often resort to desperate measures to get the drugs they need; they might even sell their own children into slavery for more drugs. They also know their children could be born addicted, and might die shortly after birth of drug withdrawal. There's also a good chance that such children will be born retarded, a common side-effect of these drugs. And there's always the consideration that drug addicts don't make very good parents.

Some people are just irresponsible, and they know it. They know they wouldn't really love their unwanted children. They may also feel that they would be just as likely to be a danger as they would to be a help. They know they won't care for such children, but can't bear the thought of giving them away, or of allowing them to grow up knowing that their parents gave them away. There are also those who feel that they can't break out of their miserable lives, and don't want to bring children into the world who will only be condemned to miserable lives themselves. These people may feel that it's better to put such unborn children out of their misery. It's also a problem when a newborn is perceived as a burden to the family. In many poor families, there's often not enough for current family members; yet another mouth to feed, or another body to clothe, may jeopardize the family's economic viability.

There are also people who will pay a young girl to become pregnant and bear a child for them. But what if she changes her mind and decides she no longer wants to have the baby? Would her "customers" be able to force her to keep it, if abortion is made illegal? Will they be able to force her to surrender the child to them?

And, last but not least, there are already quite enough abandoned children in the world. Even if it were possible to force every mother to carry every child to term, nothing can force them to care for those children properly. Far too many children have already been found dead, killed by nothing more than abandonment --- children have been found half-frozen on strangers' doorsteps. If the people of America allow the courts to make abortion illegal, this kind of thing will become much more common. It's very true that you can lead a horse to water, but you can't make it drink.

Make no mistake about it --- if we don't get the broom and the vacuum out, and clean up this world before he (Jesus) returns, we'll all pay. In the eyes of our Father in heaven, we're all brothers and sisters. We're commissioned by God to make right what we have made wrong. Passing laws that sweep the problem under the rug, and only hide the truth from open observation, will not redeem us. We will have to put our differences aside and resolve the problem, down to its root. You may not want me to be your brother, and work side-by-side to fix our world, but that won't matter to our Father on Judgment Day.

Section 15: Society Clean-Up

There are many things we can do to clean up our society. At the top of the list is our role as parents --- what parents teach their children about sex, and how, must become better defined, so that more investigative studies can be done to determine what works best to rear our children into normal and responsible sexual adults.

One way we can discover what does and doesn't work is to "anonymously" ask a full range of questions regarding how children have been raised to date. Questions about how sexual matters were dealt with by our own families should be asked, answered anonymously, and the answers analyzed. Providing anonymity will allow parents and children to contribute honest answers without fear of discovery. We can thus identify common behaviors we should engage in as well as behaviors we should avoid and discourage.

The home may be the heart of our society, but we have yet to create any formal, generally accepted method of structuring home and family life. Generation after generation is left to learn, on their own, the best way to develop children into responsible adults. We should instead have fixed, standard ways to teach our children not to lie, not to steal, not to cheat. Very little along these lines is passed on to our children to advance their upbringing; our child-rearing is mostly geared toward turning our children into workers. We teach them how to behave in group settings, how to keep themselves clean, and how to do what they're told by those in charge. We have formal ways to instill these qualities in our young, but we're all left to our own devices to teach sexual manners to our children.

The importance of abstinence is often not taught, or not taught correctly, except by churches, which obviously don't even know how to hold the interest of their congregations. The churches too often fail in their duty to give our society some sort of moral structure. Their preaching has become too dogmatic, and their messages lack substance. They should have structured activities for every stage of our lives, for home, for school, and for play (the good news is that some churches do). Even churches are becoming lax in the fight between good and evil.

In today's world of experts and specialists, we have no group of expert parents to show us proven methods of child-rearing. Dogs, cats, fish, birds --- practically all creatures of the animal kingdom --- have set, fixed ways, "as a group," of rearing their young. Why do humans, the animals with the biggest brains and most advanced minds, have no set way of rearing our young? The animals are supposedly lower forms of life, yet they have preset ways of mating and cohabiting that they knowingly (or sometimes unknowingly) follow. We, with our more developed brains, haven't been able to accomplish this feat, and our societies --- our world --- is in constant disagreement and turmoil as a result.

Perhaps we haven't learned to control these bigger brains of ours. It has been estimated that average people only use about ten percent of their brainpower, and it seems that the little part we do use is often used to lie, cheat, steal, kill, and otherwise hurt our fellow man. Little by little, day by day, we all contribute to making the human condition worse, not better. If we only devoted the same amount of energy to learning how to live well, and do better by each other, we wouldn't need half the police, or half the prisons, we have. If we used that same energy in constructive physical exercise, making money fairly, and reading, we would all be healthy, wealthy, and wise. It's a shame that, apparently since there's no financial reward in becoming a good parent, there are very few good parents around. It seems we've learned the value of money better than we've learned the value of life. As a society, we're just beginning to make an effort to limit what can and can't be legally said in the presence of children. In private, however, many adults say anything they wish to children, sometimes putting their children's mental health at risk. There are also lax standards regarding what kinds of entertainment children should or shouldn't have access to, although this is improving, with parental warning labels on music and video games.

About ninety percent of the parents in our society can't identify even one of the stages of child development, even though the vast majority of us do become parents.

As a society, we must change what television does to us, and to our children. Much of the material shown on television is sexually suggestive and encourages on-the-spot sexual arousal. Children who watch a lot of television can be influenced by that alone to become sexually promiscuous. One episode of a situation comedy clearly showed a young man under his lover's desk while she was sitting at it. He could have been looking for a contact lens, or money, but I don't think so. A commercial for Close-Up toothpaste made me wonder whether I was supposed to buy the toothpaste or get "close-up" to someone of the opposite sex. Lovemaking scenes have become a staple of nighttime soap operas, and frequently depict people making love with someone else's spouse, or with partners other than their own spouses. Even though nudity is illegal on public television, it's often implied. Television has the potential to be one of the best educational vehicles our world has to offer; instead, it's one of the worst poisoners of our minds. Thank God for PBS (the Public Broadcasting Service) stations. Without them, TV would have almost no socially redeeming value.

We need teamwork, we need teams of parents and schools and employers. Latchkey children are becoming a serious problem in our society; it has already been shown that deviant behavior and substance abuse is much greater among latchkey children. Lack of parental supervision often leads to an escalation in crime, and more. We must find a way these children can remain at school, where they can study until their parents come home. We need to develop a plan to provide childcare at our schools and places of employment. We need to find a way to supervise children, while providing them freedom, so we can carefully mold them into productive members of society, rather than just workers. Children are all too easily corrupted by unscrupulous adults; they need protection well into their adolescence. Freedom and responsibility should not be given to them suddenly, or in large proportions, but in a gradual, constructive way. What we need to determine is how much and how fast. While I don't have all the answers, I do know we must come up with the answers before too many more children are lost to the hype of sexual promiscuity.

Some might ask what this has to do with us being brothers, and what this has to do with Jesus coming back. One day, and some believe it will be soon, God will come back to us in one form or another. If you're not religious, please bear with me. When God returns, he won't be looking solely for improvements in the abortion situation --- he'll be looking at what we've done about all the evil we've hatched, raised, and grown, since he last drowned the world and all that was evil in it. We must act as brothers and sisters, to make the world ready for his return, or there will be very few of us left standing when he cleanses the world of evil again. Speaking for myself, I intend to be busy cleaning up whatever I can.

We've been ignoring the one thing that most needs cultivation. We must develop our minds beyond simple training to do a job. As our society slowly crumbles into a more and more wretched state, we must begin to fortify our minds and souls.

Section 16:

Mental

Health Plan

One segment of our society has been consistently neglected, and has never been treated with the proper respect. The mental state of our society, and of ourselves as individuals, is often ignored and overlooked. The phrase "out of sight, out of mind" is applicable, and the reasons our mental state of being is often overlooked are many. But the reason that concerns me most is our tendency to prepare ourselves only to be workers for someone else. It's so much easier to simply do what others tell us to do that we've become like sheep, following directions and achieving only the goals that make others rich. This may not be an intolerable state of affairs, as a temporary solution, a way to support ourselves. But the longer we practice this, the more we dull our mental capacities. "Out of sight, out of mind," of course, implies that we don't concern ourselves with, or worry about, things we can't see --- we can't easily see our mental abilities or perceive our mental problems, so we don't worry about these things very much. This is one of the most important reasons abortion is practiced; it's also an important reason why crime, divorce, open marriages, drug and alcohol abuse, and so on, remain common in our society.

Our society doesn't raise us to be mentally fit, or at least not to the extent that would be necessary to solve the problems of today's world. As long as we have enough sense to follow directions, well enough to hold down our jobs, we'll remain individuals on a marginal, survival footing. But for our society to do more than simply survive, we need to know more than just how to follow directions. With a structured society, and extensive rules concerning life and living, we could cut taxes in half. We pay the majority of our taxes as a kind of penalty on our incompetence and inefficiency as a society, but if we had a set way of living, if we led a clean and healthy life as a society, we wouldn't need a welfare system, a military, or prisons and law enforcement apparatus, certainly not the extensive ones we have now.

Most of our problems are caused by mental and social deficiencies. Our churches haven't been able to handle the job of keeping us on the straight and narrow, so we need, in addition, a mental health plan for our world. Without such a plan, we shouldn't believe we really can solve the problems of abortion, or racial injustice, or the greed that helps to destroy our economy, or violent crime, or any other negative societal situation.

We must take a stand against our inadequacies in dealing with our sexuality. The government has made mental health so low a priority that the government itself has become a major contributor to the problem. The government throws away billions of dollars treating the **symptoms** of our problems, and spends very little on the actual **source** of our problems. Among the avenues we should investigate, in order to solve our problems, are prayer and meditation, hypnotherapy, dream therapy, and others. We already have many techniques available to help individuals in their efforts to improve their mental well being, and I'm sure there must be many others yet to be developed.

The problem of abortion does not arise mainly from one type of deficiency, but from a wide range of personal, family, and social problems. We can beat the abortion problem --- there is a new age coming, one in which mental and spiritual growth will be at the forefront of our societies' and our governments' lists of our most urgent concerns. A time will come when big business and government will no longer be able to afford **not** to repair the damage that generations of neglect have inflicted on the peoples of the world. People's basic psychological needs will be addressed and met; we must all help if this is to work.

Mankind would probably look pretty stupid if it could be observed with a microscope. However, we as a species show much promise. Once we lived in caves, now we live in homes; once we killed each other for sport, now we have police to keep the peace; once we relied on witch doctors and shamans, now we have doctors. If we don't destroy ourselves in a moment of weakness, we'll outgrow the need for abortion. It will not need to be illegal. Little by little, day by day, we'll make it happen.

Section 17:

A Brighter Day

The day is coming when crime will be at an all-time low. War, starvation, and poverty will be things of the past. But before things get better, they're going to get worse. Our world is sinking so low that we'll be humiliated into changing our counterproductive ways. The seeds for this new age of great moral and financial wealth have already been planted, and tender but healthy sprouts are taking hold all over the world. We're learning that we haven't even begun to use the greater part of our potential for good. We use so little of our brains that it's no wonder our world is in such a mess. Millions have discovered the ease with which spiritual and mental growth can be achieved; it's only a matter of time before we make prayer and meditation a part of the school curriculum. Then we'll be only one generation away from a population of true adults. We'll be healthier, physically and mentally, than at any time in history.

You might ask, what are these tender but healthy sprouts that have taken hold? What are these signs? It's just this --- we're slowly learning that we can have complete control over our minds and bodies, and one day we'll be in control of ourselves. All our societal disasters happen because we're out of control --- we cannot or do not control our greed, sexual desires, criminal tendencies, or any other disadvantageous proclivities, not to the extent that could make a difference in reducing these problems. This is why we have so much crime, so much drug abuse, so many abortions, and so forth. Our control over ourselves is not mature yet, but for a very few dollars, we can learn the small steps that will lead us to a more complete control of our lives. Below is a list of things that can be learned and done.

1. Mental control of our blood pressure.
2. Mental control of our heart rate.
3. Mental control of our body temperature.
4. Mental control of our blood sugar levels.
5. Mental control of our brainwaves.
6. Therapeutic control of our dreams.

There are also claims that we can develop many other abilities, although these claims have yet to be substantiated. With control of our brainwaves, it's possible to reach a quietness of mind that eliminates negative thoughts; this can be brought over into our normal state of mind. This in itself could greatly help eliminate crime. We now have psychological therapies available that can help us stop smoking, stop drinking, lose weight, cope with depression, improve neurosis and psychosis, and ameliorate sexual dysfunctions of all descriptions. The problem is that we don't use these technologies and disciplines to shape our lives on a large enough scale. We seem to resort to such therapies only in case of emergencies --- so that we can get back to work. There are now machines, however, that can literally give our brains minor vacations, and speed up learning, memory, and psychological health, all at once. There has never been more information available on health and natural foods and products than there is today. The only challenge left is to use what's already known, to bring about the changes that will take us out of our adolescence and into adulthood.

I myself have been influenced by one particular type of mental discipline, meditation. It has worked a minor miracle in my life --- more than one, actually. First, meditation helped mold me into the kind of person who cares enough to write and try to reach others, and try to contribute to life in a positive way. Second, I was an atheist before I began to meditate, but meditation helped me to realize that there's something more to our existence, something more than just what this world offers. I was the worst college student of all time, and I had a fear of math that eased only after I began to meditate. I went on to pass algebra, trigonometry, and calculus. I've learned that life is truly the only important thing, whether it's this life here and now, or the life to come.

Don't ascribe any priestly or holy characteristics to me, however --- I still have an abundance of faults I must work on. But I can say without doubt that meditation has been an important help to me. And it works, without exception, for everyone. If we put meditation in our schools, it can change the moral fabric of our society. I meditate only occasionally now, out of laziness, and I only meditated regularly (as I should have) for one year. But if just one year of regular meditation can do what it did for me, what could it do for a world that regularly practices some sort of mental discipline, along with prayer? This day is coming; our good fortune is not that far away.

This is what it's all about --- sons and daughters, mothers and fathers, uncles and aunts. If we pull families apart, we take away their moral, spiritual, emotional, and financial support. Many people can make their way in the world without their families, but many cannot. And more than ever, the family is being pulled apart.

Section 18:

The Destruction of the American Family

Abortion has been with us from the beginning, but things are different today. Abortion seems to be rampant and pervasive. This is due in no small part to the disintegration of the American family, which is under attack. We should examine in some detail where this attack is originating, so let's return to the subject of latchkey children. In today's society, both parents often have to work to maintain the household. As a consequence, all over America, children have been trained to let themselves into an empty house when they come home from school, where they're on their own until a parent arrives.

It's not known how many millions of children are in this situation. But one thing is certain --- too many of these children are befriended by others, older and less innocent, who take advantage of the situation and use these children to do their bidding. Young girls, children, are becoming pregnant sometimes even before they know "the facts of life." Some become pregnant and don't even know how it happened; such girls never stood a chance. Many children are let out of the house to play, and parents often have no idea where they are. Many parents are simply unaware of the growing number of predators who use and abuse children. Even worse, there are parents who use their own children in some very strange ways.

Children are used by gangs because gangs know that children cannot be tried as adults. Other adults use children to make pornography; forty years ago, this was practically unheard of. The family is also under attack because corporate America is continually downsizing our workforce, making what was an industrial giant into a service economy. This has scrambled and scattered people all over the country, making us even more of a transient society, always surrounded by strangers. People are moving, coming and going, all the time. Families can only keep in touch via long distance, if they're to survive in today's economy. This alone has fragmented, even crippled, the extended family, and it's all due to corporate greed. The give and take of corporate entities all over the world has left the American family in disarray.

Street people are becoming an entire population unto themselves. Many street people were first dislocated from their families by job transfers, and later laid off in a downsizing, often far from their families or anyone else who might be able to help. These things are the result of corporate America's attempts to survive in today's global economy, and the sad part is that Americans continue to buy from the companies that have fallen into this trap. We should boycott companies that shuttle us around the country as if we were pawns on a chessboard, and we shouldn't buy from foreign companies when we don't have to. When we buy from companies that put their bottom line ahead of their social responsibilities, we become part of the problem.

So ultimately, the American family is under attack from itself --- we contribute to our own downfall by buying from those who dislocate people from their families by the thousands each year. This rips families apart, sometimes forever. We're "out of control" in that we don't know how this affects our own lives. So what can we do?

We must stop supporting those who contribute to the instability of family life. Buying from companies that employ cheap labor **<u>is</u>** less expensive, but we get what we pay for --- layoffs and outsourcing. We buy from cheap, greedy organizations, and we get job relocations, layoffs, downsizing, and inept management. Worse, if enough of us buy from the wrong people, we pay for it through a decline in our quality of life, the trend for many years now.

For the bigger picture, let's look at what's happening in America. Imagine that America is a single family. How is this family spending its money? And how is it destroying them? We complain about taxes and unemployment and welfare, but we create these things ourselves, by buying so many foreign-made cars and appliances that millions of jobs have been outsourced to other parts of the world. We have already given the steel and auto industries to Asia, but there would be enough jobs and education for everyone in this country if we only spent more of our money at home.

May your works in life go well.
And with no one may you be at odds.
May happiness in your family swell.
And on Judgment Day, be well with God.

Section 19: Summary

It could be that we're attacking the wrong problem. We're all trying to decide whether abortion should be legal or illegal, when in fact its legality makes no difference to a girl in trouble. A girl who may lose her home, or who may be beaten when discovered to be sexually active, knows only fear. A new law won't change this. Making abortion illegal is too simple an answer to a very complicated problem.

Most people can understand why abortion should be legal in cases of rape. After all, these poor women had little choice in bringing about their pregnancy. But some rigid, self-righteous fanatics feel that everything that happens is part of God's plan, and that women who were raped must have done something wrong to deserve it.

It's hard to understand why, of all the things that happen in this world, the Moral Majority, the Christian Coalition --- or whatever name they go by --- have chosen to focus their attention on the subject of abortion. These people don't supply or suggest ways to prevent unwanted pregnancies, but they still want to outlaw abortion. They pay taxes to a government that supports a standing army of over two million soldiers, who are prepared to kill people on a wholesale level. They want to pass a law against abortion while the rest of the world is a veritable sewer of immorality. They have their priorities confused. We must first solve the problems of those already born, those already breathing and walking among us. Then, perhaps, we'll have learned to respect each other and ourselves enough to be able to prevent unwanted pregnancies before they occur. It's not the act of abortion itself we need to change, it's not the actions of doctors we need to circumscribe, it's not a new law we need to pass. It's our mental maturity we must change.

America is the greatest country; our sciences and businesses have advanced at an incredible rate. But there's an area we've ignored, and because we've ignored it, the fabric of our society is disintegrating. The only way we'll ever put a stop to the sickness of abortion is to make new strides in our mental development. We must be in the right frame of mind, as individuals and as a society, or we'll always have unwanted pregnancies and abortions.

The minds of our young women have been filled with garbage. Television, radio, and billboards on the highways all depict women as sexual entertainment for men, and women in advertisements are almost always suggestively dressed. Young women brought up today are in deep trouble --- the role models they view as successful are usually nothing more than "treats" for men. It's also important that our criminal justice system doesn't sufficiently punish adults who push very young girls and boys into becoming sexually active. Two thirds of all **underage** girls who become pregnant are impregnated by adult men, men over 18. Pedophiles run rampant in America, molesting children and turning them into sexual deviants. This must be stopped. Young girls who are lured off playgrounds to satisfy the needs of sexual deviants should not be required to bear the children of those perpetrators.

The people who will be most affected by a law banning abortion are the workers and the poor. The rich will simply go to Canada or Mexico, or wherever abortion might be legal, safe, and clean. In the battle for souls, the battle between the forces of good and evil, more souls will be lost to the dark side if abortion is made illegal, because we would no longer have records of how many people seek abortions and how many obtain them. A few people will be jailed, and the problem will be considered solved. We have the ugly monster, abortion, out in the open now; this may be our only chance to get a good grip on it.

Why should we create another business for organized crime to exploit? We all know that if there's a demand for a service, someone will provide it. As soon as abortions are made illegal, an underworld of medical school dropouts and quacks will start up new businesses to meet the demand. What sense does it make to enable this?

The only reason the pro-life movement has gotten as far as it has is because of the way people vote. The Moral Majority (or the Christian Coalition) wanted their issues to become important in American politics, and the Republican Party said they would help them accomplish this. The Republicans always knew they could not really bring it about, but in the meantime, they have ruled American politics for almost two decades, relying on the people's belief in their empty, sick promise. The Christian Coalition apparently took no notice of the fact that neither abortion nor prayer in schools was even addressed in Newt Gingrich's

"Contract with America." They only want votes, and will misrepresent their positions in order to get them.

I do believe, however, that one day, when we have matured as a race, we'll outgrow this kind of behavior. We won't need a law against abortion, and there will no longer be abortionists. Until then, let's keep abortion exposed to our scrutiny and not sweep it under the rug. The more we know about it, the better we can fight it.

Thank you for your time. May God bless us all.

We have to bring jobs back to America. Corporate will not do it. The government is being paid off by corporate so they will not do it. That leaves you and I. This and other answers are in this book.

We have been on the small government kick for about 30 years now. This book tells you why it has all been a hoax and how our congressmen has been turned into sock puppets for the rich.

www.ingramcontent.com/pod-product-compliance
Lightning Source LLC
LaVergne TN
LVHW010626100826
845148LV00014B/3134

* 9 7 8 0 6 1 5 3 5 7 0 3 4 *